Clipping, Trimming and Plaiting Your Horse

Diana R. Tuke

J. A. Allen

London

British Library Cataloguing in Publication Data
Tuke, Diana R. (Diana Rosemary), 1932–
    Clipping, trimming and plaiting your horse.
    2nd rev ed
    I. Title
    636.10833

    ISBN 0851315380

Published in Great Britain by
J. A. Allen & Company Limited,
1, Lower Grosvenor Place, Buckingham Palace Road,
London, SW1W OEL

Illustrations, Maggie Raynor

Typeset in Hong Kong by Setrite Typesetters Ltd.
Printed in Hong Kong by Dah Hua Printing Co. Ltd.

Front and Back Cover Illustrations

Front

Lister's Showman (right), Stablemate (centre) and Laser (left)

Wolseley's Harrier (left), Swift (centre), Falcon (right).

Lister Showman clippers running off a deluxe battery back pack, giving the finishing touches. Note the safety loop over the wrist, and the blanket over the mare's back to prevent chilling. Also the tail is plaited and bandaged to keep it clear of her hind legs.

Lister showman clipper. Note the mane bunched in elastic bands to clear the neck and allow free movement of clippers over neck.

Cleaning the back of the clipper blades with a small brush. Note grooved blades, fitted to Lister clippers, which prevent clogging.

After clipping, a horse must be warmly rugged correctly. Here we have a Thermalite Flectron-filled nylon rug with a cotton lining. Underneath is worn a yellow wool blanket over a cotton summer sheet, with a Union-web roller over a shaped foam pad to prevent pressure on the withers and spine.

Back

Equipment assembled for clipping. Lister's Showman clippers in case; oil; brushes; spare blades; battery; elastic bands; tail bandage; grooming kit; rug/blanket; handclippers; and adjustable headcollar.

Plaiting the mane. Sewing the first plait, with the next plaited ready for sewing and the rest in bunches awaiting plaiting.

Thermal, waterproof, exercise rug made to the author's design by Bryan Lawrence.

Shires', fleece-lined Storm Cheeter New Zealand rug, with hind leg straps and crossed surcingles; note the correct crossing of the straps. Also, as the mare had been freshly turned out, Woof boots for safety.

Removing a section of mane over the poll to allow the bridle to rest comfortably. First prototype of the excellent new Wolseley trimming clippers being evaluated.

Preparing to plait and trim. Stable rubber, water brush, clothes peg (to take cut lengths of cotton ready for sewing up), reel of thick thread, comb for plaiting and dog comb for pulling tail, elastic bands, tin of needles and scissors. Double-blunt scissors are also required for removing plaits.

Contents

List of Illustrations

Acknowledgements
(First edition)

I am indebted to the following companies for their help in obtaining the necessary photographs and illustrations for this book: W. G. Hayes and Sons Limited, Saddlers, 6, Dyer Street, Cirencester, Gloucestershire; R. A. Lister Farm Equipment Limited, Dursley, Gloucestershire; Wolseley Engineering Produts, H. Cameron Gardner Limited, Bath Road, Woodchester, Stroud, Gloucestershire. Also to Mrs. James Greenwell who gave up much of her time to help me with River Gipsy, my own thoroughbred, when we had her chaser clipped as a four-year-old. And last but not least, to River Gipsy herelf. By River Poaching out of Galavant, homebred, foaled July, 1977, she has been a most willing model. As a four-and-a-half-year-old, she let us reclip her for this book although confined for many weeks to her box following a serious accident, in which she severed an artery in her off-fore. By keeping the leg clipped out as described in this book, the injury has healed without mark. Just after her fifth birthday it was discovered she had very serious, long standing anaemia from a virus and was also losing the sight of her right eye. Her sight has now returned, her blood is excellent and, at the time of writing, gun-shot pellets that landed in her while she was out to grass as a three-year-old are coming out, hence the reason as a six-year-old she is clipped out to let us find them.

To the University of Bristol School of Veterinary Science, Langford, Somerset, who examined her in late October, and to her Veterinary Surgeon, Mr. Peter Bown, B.V.M.S., F.R.C.V.S., River Gipsy and I owe a very special thank you, for I transferred her to the care of the George Veterinary Group, Malmesbury, Wiltshire, in December when there was little hope for her sight — they fought and they won.

Acknowledgements (Second edition)

Nearly a decade on from the first edition, I wish to thank, not only those who helped me with the first edition, but also the following for their help in updating this edition: Bartlow Saddlery and Country Sports Ltd., The Kennels, Hadstock Road, Bartlow, Cambs., CB1 6PW, for allowing me to photograph the only clippers whose photographs were not supplied by the firm; Brookwich Ward & Co. Ltd., 88 Westlaw Place, Whitehill Estate, Glenrothes, Fife, KY62 R2, for information on the Huptner Electric Rapide; Equequip Ltd., Fox Barn, Banbury Road, Moreton Pinkney, Daventry, Northants; NN11 6SQ, for information and photographs; Mrs Georgena Kirkland, who not only very kindly allows River Gipsy to spend her summers in her paddock and stables, in the greatest comfort, but also took some of the photographs; Lister Shearing Equipment Ltd., Dursley, Glos., GL11 4HR, for all their help once again in supplying clippers, information and photographs; Liveryman, Eddie Palin Distribution Ltd., Chester Road, Tern Hill, Market Drayton, Shropshire, TF9 2JQ, for their help with information and photographs; Stock-Shop Wolseley, Clyst Honiton, Exeter, Devon, EX5 2LJ, for all their help with information (even coming up to visit me in East Anglia), photographs, and clippers, and for letting me try the first prototype of their new clippers; my nephew Richard Tuke for taking most of the cover photographs and some of the text photographs. I could not have managed without him. It is nice to have the next generation helping me with my books — Richard's father having taken many of the photographs for my earlier ones; and lastly, but by no means least, River Gipsy herself — 14 this July. These photographs were taken in 1990 and 1991, and once again she gave her full cooperation. On leaving the Cotswolds we could not part with her, so she came too, spending the summers here with us in a friend's field and stable, and the winters at livery because we no longer have anywhere of our own for her.

D. R. T. June 1991

Preface

Nature provided the equine race with warm coats to protect them in the cold weather and thinner ones for the warmer months. This is fine — so long as a horse or pony is not going to be required to undertake any fast work when carrying a full winter coat. Few owners however, wish to rest their horses and ponies in winter, expecting them, on the contrary, to gallop and jump across country, or work hard in a covered school. However fit they may be, under such conditions a horse or pony will sweat and often become dripping wet, taking hours to dry off once work has ceased. In order to maintain their condition, allow them to dry quickly and avoid undue stress, their coats, whole or in part, must be removed and replaced by rugs in the stable and at slow exercise.

The removal of a horse's winter coat is no recent innovation: our forefathers, needing to travel faster and liking to hunt, removed the coats of their horses; initially either by shaving or singeing and, later, by clipping with hand clippers. Hand-turned power clippers were introduced — some of which are still in use to this day — to which a motor was then added and these same machines became our power-driven clippers on a tripod. Electric clippers soon followed and today there are many different makes to choose from. One person alone nowadays can clip a horse, if of course, it is quiet, and with manpower at a premium, this is indeed a blessing.

In this book I intend to look at, and explain, clipping in depth, so as to enable the ordinary owner or groom to do a workmanlike job. Good clipping is a pleasure to see, bad clipping an eyesore.

Why Clipping is Necessary

Though a horse sweats in its summer coat, this is neither dangerous nor even a hazard to its well being. The temperature in summer is such that the horse is less likely to chill while drying off, and a short summer coat dries quickly. Winter weather is, of course, far colder, and once hot the horse will stay wet or damp, as its winter coat, long, dense and full of grease, holds moisture, making it cold and very likely to take chill.

Sweating also takes condition from a horse, making it hard to keep enough flesh on its body, However much you feed a horse, it may still lose condition − that is, lose weight and grow thin − leaving it vulnerable to any infection that might be around, for its resistance which is so essential to good health, has been lowered to a point beyond which infection cannot be kept at bay.

In order to maintain health and condition, a horse must be thoroughly groomed and the pores of its skin kept open to allow the free extrusion of sweat. A horse carrying a full winter coat cannot be so thoroughly groomed, will be uncomfortable when hot and sweaty, and, thus, more likely to fidget.

Rain too, makes a horse with a long coat far harder to dry off, while rain and sweat mixed is very sticky and can stay damp for hours.

In order to combat the above and enable a horse to carry out fast work over a much longer period of time, without detriment either to its health or performance, it is customary to remove all or some of the winter coat − sometimes the summer coat too, if it is coarse and the horse has to work hard − and replace the missing coat with rugs to maintain warmth.

Once clipped a horse can be worked thoroughly and groomed to maintain good health.

It is usual to clip in the autumn, sometime in October, depending on the horse's coat and the weather, and then approximately once every month or six weeks. Some people only clip about three times during the winter, but I prefer never to let the horse's coat grow to any length: chilling is far more likely to occur if a horse, having become accustomed to its regrown coat, suddenly loses it again. Far better to keep it short by more frequent clipping.

The last clip of the winter depends on whether the horse is being used for competition work or not and on when hunting stops in the district concerned. It has been suggested that a horse's coat does not grow properly if clipped late but no hard-and-fast rule has been established on this. In fact, many show horses are clipped right out in early spring just prior to shedding, in order to bring their show coats through for the early shows.

A clipped coat saves endless time to an owner and distress to a horse, but do ensure that you have enough rugs — at least three for severe weather — before clipping your horse, and that they are warm and fit properly.

Choosing Clippers

Before starting to clip you must decide which type of clipper to purchase. The choice is fairly wide. Nowadays the majority are electric, though it is still possible to purchase those designed to run from the vacuum pipes of a milking unit, besides, of course, the hand-operated ones.

Early electric clipper models were normally known as pendant or portable; they can still be obtained. The pendant model has a ¼ horsepower large motor which hangs from the ceiling on a special bracket and has a flexible head. The portable model has the motor fitted to a tripod, and is very similar to the old hand-turned clippers where a helper turned a handle that drove the shaft that moved the blades. This model also has a fuel motor. For many years, the pendant and portable models were the ones most usually found. The hand grip was narrow and they did a competent job, though the user was very restricted by the shaft. Also they were not as quiet as the clippers which house the motor in a combined handle and head. Both Wolseley's and Lister's make these models.

These two companies have always run close in clipper manufacture, the main difference lying in design of the heads and blades.

For those people with several horses to clip, a larger heavy-duty type of electric clipper is probably the answer, especially if horses with thick coats are to be clipped. It will glide more swiftly through the coat than a lighter model, as the motor, housed in the handle, is larger and more powerful. Men normally find this model preferable, but women, whose hands tend to be smaller, often find the lighter models easier to use.

In the heavy-duty range are those clippers that come in the

Lister's Laser — heavy duty.

220–240 volt, 50 cycle (50 HZ) AC or DC 100–150 watts range; a few models are only 80 watts, but are still classed as heavy duty.

The following clippers all have similar motors, but their heads and blades vary considerably to give the owner a wide choice: of the older models we have Wolseley Princess de Luxe, the Lister Supreme, the Lister Premier 2, Equequip, Hauptner, Sunbeam Stewart, the Clipmaster and Variable Speed Clipmaster (the last two both from Sunbeam Stewart), Eider Kombi, Aesculap Econom and the Euroclipper with its 160 watt motor.

By the start of the 1990s a new family of clippers had come on the market to join their fellows: Lister's new mains clippers were headed by their 170 watt Laser, with Stablemate (45 watt) replacing the Premier. Stablemate is much more sophisticated than its predecessor, having a unique design of a ventilated head that blows the hair away from the user and the blades. Equequip have two new models: the Professional, boasting a 220 watt motor, and Handy-Clipper (120 watt). Hauptner's now have the 160 watt Electric-Rapide, while Wolseley, now under new management, have no fewer than three new models with which to challenge their competitors. The Falcon heads the range with a 170 watt motor, the Harrier comes next with

4

Wolseley's Harrier – heavy duty, Swift which replaces the old Pedigree, and Falcon – medium.

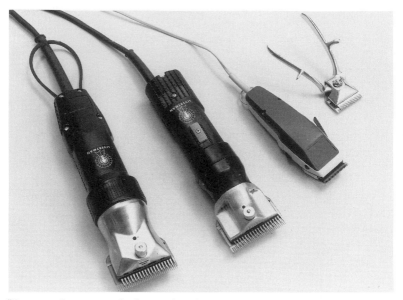

Liveryman's range – the heavy duty Leader, lightweight Arena, with their trimmer Companion, and handclipper

150 watts and the old Pedigree is replaced by the 75 watt Swift. These well-known companies have now been joined by Liveryman, a firm started after the old Wolseley changed ownership. The Liveryman range has two main models: the 150 watt Leader and the very light (1 kg) 90 watt Arena. The Wolseley and Liveryman blades are interchangeable. Robinsons also market Heiniger Handy Clipper (120 watt), and like Equequip have a Voltage Speed Controller to reduce speed, noise, etc. for when working round the ears and eyes.

In the medium range are two of the most widely-used models: the old Wolseley Pedigree and the Lister Premier. These clippers are light, quiet and compact, a delight to use. The Lister model has an all metal head, whereas the Wolseley has a nylon one, rendering it the lighter of the two. The Wolseley also has a safety handle, useful should you accidentally let go of the clippers while in use. The Wolseley Pedigree is also available in the form of Pedigree 2, which has a motor giving 50 per cent more power and a slimmer, better-balanced handle, but still remaining reasonably quiet when running, a characteristic that

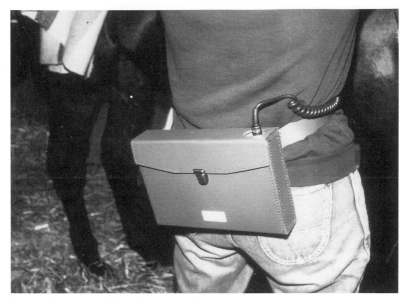

Lister's Showman deluxe battery pack

made the earlier model such a first-class clipper to use, even on thoroughbreds. My own thoroughbred, River Gipsy, made no fuss whatsoever when clipped for the first time as a four-year-old, with the old-style Pedigree. The Pedigree 2, does have a slight increase in noise and air filter draught caused by the extra power and speed of the blades. The motors of the Lister Premier 1, and the Wolseley Pedigree 1 (old models), were in the 200–250 volt AC or DC, 40 watts category and are still available, though mainly now as second-hand models. The Wolseley Pedigree 2 is 65 watts.

In a class of its own comes the Lister Lo-Volt safety clipper. Now beige in colour instead of orange and named the Showman. Fitted with AC fine blades as standard it gives an outstanding, clean, smooth clip and is a pleasure to use. Thanks to the up-graded motor, it is very easy to operate and maintain. Only 12 volts, it works off either a rechargeable battery pack strapped to the user's back, from a 12-volt car battery or off the mains via a mains adaptor. I now use this clipper with a battery pack and find it not only quick to use, but light and cool in the hand, and particularly useful on horses that move about, as they cannot get a leg over the lead, nor is there a risk if the horse decides to bite the lead. If clippers are connected to the mains this is a real danger, but with a battery pack no harm would result except to the clipper lead. For those with no power laid on, the battery pack or car 12-volt battery models are a real asset. Two rechargeable battery packs are now available; the original de luxe model and the recent basic model.

Of the smaller American clippers, the Andis Power Groomer has a wide 'T' blade for clipping the whole of the horse's body, and narrower blades which include an ear/fetlock blade and a blade with extra fine teeth for very close clipping required before an operation. Andis also produce a Groom Clipper that changes the cutting depths from fine to coarse at the flick of a switch. Their ear clippers are very quiet, especially good for those horses that hate having their ears clipped, while the Andis cordless, adjustable clipper comes with its own charger. The Andis Tack-Mate has a fixed blade for the heads and ears.

Oster's range includes small trimming clippers, an ear clipper and an animal trimmer, the Raycine ear trimmer, and some larger models of 35 watts, 115 volts or 120 volts according to model. The lower voltage is for smaller animals, while the 120-volt clippers come with wide blades for fast clipping. The Rex and Sunbeam Delta Trimmers also fall into this range.

Trimming clippers have come a long way in recent years. They include a battery-model companion to Moser's Rex; the Primat Akku (rechargeable); Primat Cordless; Maxicut Cordless; Minicut Cordless; Wahl (U.S.A.) Cordless (battery); and Liveryman Companion. In addition Moser now have a powerful motor-driven 30 watt small clipper the Professional, and Wahl's Multi-Cut is another mains trimmer.

Many of the trimming clippers, are in fact, dog clippers, but Wolseley are launching a rechargeable trimmer, made expressly for horses, and the first prototype has thrilled me. Named the Skylark, it is quiet, a delight to handle, comes with a variety of blades — from veterinary to hunter — to match other clippers, and is ideal for heads, heels, veterinary work etc. Gipsy has even permitted me to do her ears with it, in addition to whiskers, poll and withers.

Lastly, there are hand clippers. Lister's hand clipper has

8

Lister's grooved blades: CA2 coarse blade (top) − A2 medium blade (left) − A2F fine blade, now fitted as standard (right) − AC top blade (bottom). Base plate fits all.

blades like an electric clipper, coarser but not too coarse, that are operated with one hand. I have had a pair since 1951 which I would not be without; I use them for all fetlock trimming, and such jobs as taking out the small section of mane behind the ears and over the withers, and trimming the jaws in summer. Easy to use, every tack box should contain a pair, or the similar type made by Equequip. Hauptner produce a double-handed version that has proper blades, and can be obtained with straight or side cut, but having used this type many years ago for hogging ponies (we sat on the pony's back and worked up from the withers!), I find the single-handed model like a barber's clipper, preferable every time. Hauptner also make a hand clipper for use with one hand, but it works on the principle of a single blade passing over the lower blade of teeth like a sheep shear, with far sharper points that could prick the horse.

Clipper blades come in a variety of thicknesses and with different numbers of teeth. It is the bottom blade, or comb, that denotes the thickness of the clip. The standard horse

9

blades are normally A2 for the bottom blade and A3 for the top blade; Lister clippers are A2F for finer blades. Wolseley have only one number: A2 indicates fine plates for horse clipping, while the top blade has no separate number. A6 is their coarse blade for cattle clipping and this can be used on a horse's legs if coarse clipping is required. Lister's cattle blades carry the code A1 for the top blade and CA2 for the bottom. Hauptner's range of large clippers now covers six types — hunter as before, fine for thoroughbreds, very fine for veterinary use, coarse for ponies and moorland breeds, thick for cattle and a very thick plucking blade for hogged manes etc. They are interchangeable with the Euroclipper, Sunbeam and Lister Supreme, as are the Liveryman and Wolseley blades interchangeable. Equequip normally come with fine blades, but can be fitted with hunter blades which are slightly coarser. The American clippers come with their own sizing; in the range of blades by Oster there are regular, skip-tooth, blocking, and special, while the Andis range includes the 'T' blade, ear/fetlock, surgical and the GC which are grooved at their base. This grooved base is also found on the new Lister blades as it reduces weight and allows the hair to glide more freely through the teeth, leading to swifter, cleaner clipping. All other models have their own blades, or in a few cases are made to use those of another firm. Never mix blades or use them on a make other than that which the manufacturers state may be used. Remember they are designed for use with a certain type of clipper only, so stick to the correct blades for your model.

The choice of clipper blades depends on what you require of your horse. If you are not going to do any fast work, do not clip too close, but if you are going to stable your horse all the time and exercise with a rug on in cold weather, use a finer blade. I like fine blades, providing they do not clip skin tight. Wolseley A2 and Lister's grooved blades give a nice clean clip that is fine but not skinned.

Today clippers are packed in hard cases with the necessary items like oil and cleaning brushes included, which is an excellent thing, because it protects the clipper, keeps it dry and makes transporting it far easier than of old. Having chosen your clipper, take care of it.

3 Maintaining Clippers

Clipping machines are both expensive and, if not properly maintained, potentially lethal, especially if they are electric. Therefore, treat clippers carefully and look after them correctly. Sound maintenance is essential for safety and good clipping. New clippers will arrive from the manufacturers with full instructions as to how to use and care for the model concerned. Read these very carefully and keep the instruction leaflet or booklet in a safe place for future reference. Each model varies slightly in its make-up, but certain rules apply to all clippers. At all times electric clippers — and others for that matter — must be kept quite dry: never leave them in a damp stable or unheated tack room. Instead, store them in a dry, damp-free place in the house, where there is no risk of them being dropped or knocked. If allowed to become damp, the electric motor will become dangerous and the metal parts rust.

Never use clippers near water or hold them in water; nor should you handle clippers while turning a tap on or off (these warnings are printed in the leaflets that come with American clippers).

Never leave clippers out of doors or place on a damp surface, and avoid steam.

When not in use, clippers must be kept well oiled and greased for protection.

Whether oiling clippers and their blades (plates) for storage or for use, a good quality thin oil must be used — SAE 5, R 15, or similar oil. Some clippers come with their own oil, but thin 3-in-One oil may also be used, but be sure it is suitable for electric machines. Special clipper oil,' which cools and cleans the clippers while in use, and is medicated to help prevent

11

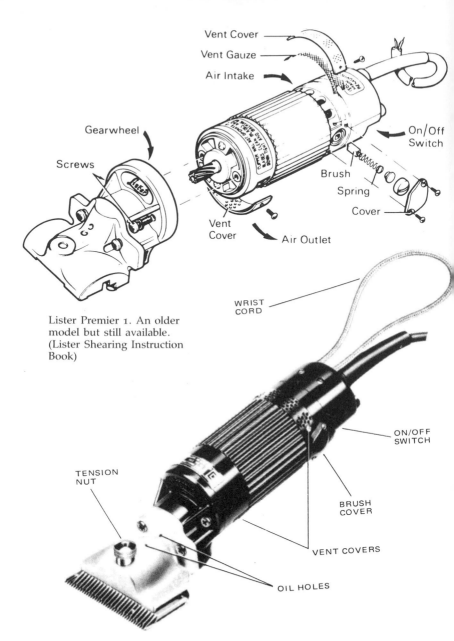

Vent Cover

Vent Gauze

Air Intake

Gearwheel

Screws

On/Off Switch

Brush

Spring

Cover

Vent Cover

Air Outlet

WRIST CORD

Lister Premier 1. An older
model but still available.
(Lister Shearing Instruction
Book)

ON/OFF SWITCH

TENSION NUT

BRUSH COVER

VENT COVERS

OIL HOLES

Wolseley Pedigree 1 with A2 blades. The forerunner of the Pedigree 2 where
the on/off switch is located on top of the motor. (Wolseley Operators
Handbook)

1 Clipper wiring label
2 Clipper label
3 Clipper specification label 220-240V
  Clipper specification label 110-115V
4 Gearbox assembly
  (Comprising items 9 & 10)
5 Motor 220-240V
  Motor 110-115V
6 Head assembly
  (Comprising items 15−22)
7 Head retaining screw
8 Washer
9 Plain bearing
10 Gearbox seal
11 Tension bolt
12 Tension nut
13 Tension spring

14 Blades
15 Clipper head
16 Needle bearing
17 Bearing
18 Gear & shaft assembly
19 Crank head
20 Crank roller
21 Crank roller spring
22 Comb peg
23 Blade protector

Lister Laser

13

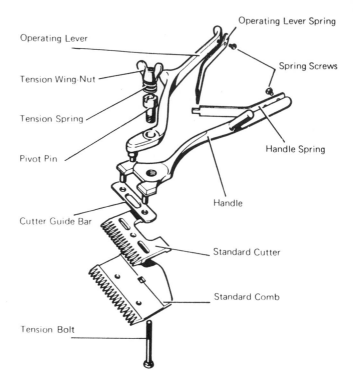

Operating Lever

Operating Lever Spring

Tension Wing-Nut

Spring Screws

Tension Spring

Handle Spring

Pivot Pin

Cutter Guide Bar

Handle

Standard Cutter

Standard Comb

Tension Bolt

Handclipper

clipper rash, is now easy to obtain in either aerosol cans with long thin nozzles that make easy the oiling of the clipper blades and head holes, or squeeze bottles. If you use an aerosol ensure it does not evaporate thereby leaving no oil; test by spraying it on the index finger, leave for five minutes, then rub the finger with the thumb. It should still be really oily, if it is not, do not use it because it will damage the clippers, and blades. Incidentally, the old habit of running clipper blades in paraffin, surgical spirit, or, worst of all, diesel oil (the latter being extremely detrimental to the clippers) should not be practised under any circumstances.

When oiling clippers, place a few drops in the holes provided on the clipper head. Oil is essential as clippers have moving parts which must be kept lubricated otherwise they will overheat when running.

Cleaning the latest generation of Wolseley clippers; removing the head from the Harrier.

Brushing out the hairs from the head.

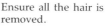

Ensure all the hair is removed.

Next turn the clipper round and remove the cover from the air vent and brush out any dust and hair that might be there.

When the clippers are reassembled, oil thoroughly

The air vent on the Falcon is on top. The head is left on for normal cleaning.

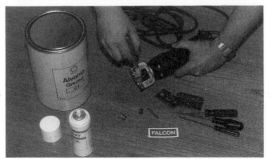

Next clean out the head thoroughly having removed the blades.

Finally, oil — remember to shake the can before use.

The Swift requires similar treatment to the Falcon.

Grease is required for the inside of the gear casing. This houses the gearwheel that drives the clippers. After every 100 hours of use and at the start of every clipping season, remove the clipper head by undoing the two screws that hold it to the body of the clipper. Clean out any old grease carefully and check the gearwheel for wear or broken teeth — if damaged, get them repaired before further use. Once the old grease has been removed repack the case using clean grease — Shell Alvania 2 is the type used by most clipper manufacturers, but it is not easy to obtain in some districts, so an equivalent must be used — Castrol LM Grease is one that comes in a suitably sized tin. Motor shops are normally suppliers of this type of grease, but *never* use graphite molybdenum or other electrically conductive greases as these could interfere with the double insulation of the clippers. Having repacked the gear casing, screw it back on to the clipper body. Run for a short time and wipe away any grease that comes out of the oil holes.

No owner should tamper with the electric motor: the only parts that may be touched when the clipper is disconnected — *never* when in use — are the brushes which require checking initially after 100 hours and subsequently after every 50 hours in use; they should be renewed if worn to five millimetres. Use the correct type of brush and spring — Nobrac Grade C.565 or equivalent in the case of the Wolseley Pedigree — but check with the makers if in any doubt, as failure to use the correct brushes could cause damage to the armature. If, when running, the motor is thought to be slow or is overheating, then return it to the makers for checking, having first made sure that the clipper blades have not been overtensioned, that lubrication has been carried out and that the electricity supply is of the correct voltage for the particular clipper model being used.

It is also essential to ensure that the air vents are kept clean. Those clippers with vent covers and vent gauze must have the covers and gauze removed and the hair and dust blown out of the recesses but do *not* poke it out as this could damage the clippers. Replace the gauze and cover. The screws that hold the cover are tiny, so remove them over a piece of paper and make sure you do not lose them. Clean after every clipping.

The heavy-duty lead that connects the clippers to the mains electricity supply must be checked for damage before every clipping. Never let a horse tread on the lead − if it does so, switch off and do not use again until the lead has been renewed. Internal damage cannot be seen and the risk is too great. Check the plug too − the nonbreakable kind are the safest. Use only fused plugs with a 2 amp fuse though up to 5 amp is safe in some machines. If in any doubt, use the lower amp. Most clippers are double insulated and therefore must not be earthed. When fitting the plug ensure that no lead is connected to the earth unless an earth lead is specifically called for, and follow the wiring code very carefully. If in any doubt get a qualified electrician to fit the plug and check the brushes for you.

Clipper blades, or plates, are delicate pieces of precision engineering. Some forty different processes are involved in the manufacture of clipper blades, including, to name but a few, blanking, drilling, milling, grinding, heat treatment, polishing and lapping − the latter process ensures both cutter and comb match as a pair and finish to a fine degree. Both new blades and those returned for regrinding − sharpening − should be lapped to get a perfect finish on both blades. Therefore when sending your blades for resharpening, ensure that they go to a reputable firm, or back to the makers. (Stock-Shop Wolseley now do my blades.) The blades come in matched pairs, each pair being ground to work only with its partner to ensure that the blades are kept in their original pairs and never mixed up. The best way to keep the blades when not in use is in the

A modern lapping machine at Wolseley's new factory.

plastic two-sided case provided with many (but not all) of the makes. The blades should be inserted teeth first with their face turned inwards so that when the folder is shut the two flat surfaces come together, separated only by the case. Made of specially hardened steel for good cutting qualities, the teeth will break if knocked or dropped.

Before putting clipper blades away, clean well and then oil. As I am very conscious of the risk of passing skin infection from one horse to another, I always wash my blades after use in warm Savlon, rinse well and dry, then place carefully in a warm place until they are completely dry. Then I make sure they are well oiled and stored away until next required. This washing removes all dirt from the teeth and I have never found it to affect the cutting edge. Having removed the blades from the clipper head to clean and store them, wipe out all loose hair from the inside of the head — a tissue works very well — being careful not to lose the drive end bearing ring that fits inside the top blade. To hold this ring in place when the blades are not attached, place a small piece of foam over the end. Also, remember to replace the tension screw — with its spring and nut — in its hole to prevent loss. I never leave blades on clippers as they are too vulnerable (though with modern cases it is possible); once the teeth get broken, they are useless and dangerous.

When fitting the blades to the clipper head make sure the top blade — cutter — is correctly fitted before adding the bottom blade — comb — and pass the tension screw through the hole from the bottom. Next, place the spring, if not attached to the nut, over the screw on top of the head and lastly the nut. Screw down to finger tight and slacken off. *Never* use a wrench or pliers. The correct tension is essential and varies from make to make — from half a turn to one and a half turns — but the best results are obtained by reading the instructions (though you can rely on the engine noise to tell you if the machine is running freely and easily). Too tight and the motor and blades will overheat; too slack and hair will get stuck between the blades and cause drag. Either will wreck the clippers and make the horse very clipper-shy, so care for your clippers correctly and treat them sensibly and with respect.

New or reground blades must be wiped completely clean to remove the protective rust inhibitor (otherwise it will burn on and stop the blades from cutting) and be oiled before being used.

Adjust the tension of hand clippers by pressing both handles together, tightening the wing nut to fix them; then, holding the right handle only, release the nut till the handles spring apart, adding another half turn before oiling.

Types of Clip

Before beginning to clip a horse it is essential to know exactly what clip to adopt. The type of clip depends very largely on the work required of your horse, and how you are going to keep it.

Those horses called on to work hard and fast will require more of their coat removed than those doing only slow work or work that entails much standing about.

Horses of a plebeian nature carry far denser and coarser coats than their better-bred counterparts; the former will probably need clipping right out at the start of the winter, whereas those with fine coats will often benefit from having part of the coat left on to protect their backs from extreme cold.

The basic five types of clip are: full, hunter, blanket, chaser and trace.

Full

As the name implies, a full clip means the removal of the entire coat, save for a very neat inverted 'V' above the tail. Care must be exercised not to clip into the mane, unless this is to be hogged off too. Horses are certainly much easier to clean when clipped right out and injuries are easier to spot and treat. This is a very sensible clip for autumn as it prevents excessive sweating on those late autumn days when coats have almost grown and horses are not yet fully fit. In the summer too, many horses that carry a dense summer coat benefit from being clipped right out for showing or competition work, though it is to be stressed that clipping show horses must be done as soon as the summer coat comes through and repeated

Full clip

to prevent it looking clipped. Strictly speaking they are not clipped, but shown with summer coats which have been produced by heavy rugging to look short and sleek. Clipping does however enable some whose coats are heavy all year round, to lead a more comfortable life.

Hunter

The hunter clip is similar to a full clip in so far as the body, head and neck are clipped out, but a patch of long hair is left

Hunter clip

for protection against scalding under the saddle and the legs are left for warmth and protection against thorns. True, the saddle patch is an asset for a cold-backed horse, but I have found with a numnah — and many saddles require one — that the cold-back question does not arise. Clipped out, the back dries faster (though care must be exercised to ensure it is not left uncovered while hot, or chilling will result). As for scalding or rubbing, I have had as much trouble with unclipped backs as with clipped ones, but I would add that if you are going to remove the saddle patch, then a numnah must be used to protect the back. As for legs, too much hair can hide injuries and thorns until they fester and the horse goes lame. Heels too, if left untouched, harbour more trouble than they save. A compromise is to clip right out the first time and hunter clip thereafter. Thus the horse gets the best of both worlds: it has some hair on its legs to keep it warm in the winter, but not enough to hide trouble.

Blanket

The blanket clip is very useful for horses that are to be stabled at night, but run out by day in a New Zealand rug. The hair is removed from the lower part of the body and hindquarters, up as far as the root of the tail and from the head, neck and chest; the legs are left unclipped and so too is the back for protection

Blanket clip

and warmth. If done neatly and well, it can look very acceptable and workmanlike. The corners should be rounded and a half-circle removed over the flank, where the horse sweats most. Some people like to clip straight lines and squared-off corners as it is easier, but this is, to my mind, very ugly, and not nearly as effective. The front of the clip should follow the line of the saddle, as for a saddle patch in a hunter clip. It is actually a saddle patch with the area left over the loins and quarters for added protection against chilling. A horse's loins are very vulnerable to chill, so this is a useful clip in the autumn for horses that run out by day and, for horses that hunt, it is useful during cubbing, because standing about at the covertside can be very chilling indeed. A full or hunter clip can then be given for the opening meet after which the horses will be stabled day and night.

Chaser

Though similar to a blanket clip, the chaser clip leaves hair on the neck in addition to the back, to protect the muscles up the sides of the neck. This proves useful on well-bred horses that tend to have back trouble. The line up either side of the neck is terminated at the ears, where the bridle rest is clipped out. It is clip I have used over a number of years on my thoroughbreds, its name echoing its popularity as a clip for steeplechasers.

Chaser clip

Trace

The trace clip has several variations: high, medium and low, the latter being useful for children's ponies who are only being worked at weekends and in the school holidays. As the name implies, the horse is clipped to the height of the traces, for this was a clip used on harness horses, rather than riding horses, though now it is used for both. The head, neck and back are left unclipped, and so too are the legs. The hair on the underside of the jaw, the windpipe and the chest between the legs is

High trace clip

Medium trace clip

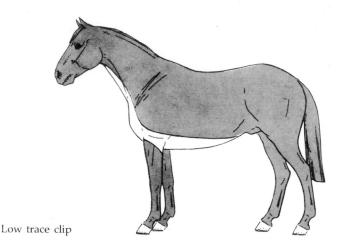

Low trace clip

removed — in some cases with a medium or high clip (dis-
cussed later) — as is the hair on the lower part of the shoulders
through to the hindquarters including the underside of the
belly. Where the coat is removed under the belly using a
medium or high — but not a low — clip, the clip will include a
narrow run up either side to the root of the tail. With the low
clip, the lower part of the shoulders above the elbows is removed, but in some cases the hindquarters are left completely.
A high trace clip is much the same as the chaser, but the head
is left unclipped too. This is also a useful clip for ponies, but
I prefer a chaser for horses if they will permit their heads
to be clipped!

These are the different types of clip: choose the one most
suited to your horse and its work.

Clipping Your Horse

Clipping is an art, but an art that can be acquired if approached with commonsense and careful thought before undertaking the job.

First, check your clippers are in sound working order — greased and oiled ready for use and running smoothly with no chance of causing a shock. Next check that you have two pairs of sharp blades belonging to the clippers you are going to use. Makes vary, so I repeat, do not try to use blades made for one make on clippers of another make.

Next, the place where you are going to clip must be prepared. Ideally, a spare box with a good light and power-point (for electric clippers) at a convenient height, because the floor will be dry and free of bedding. Remember, when clipping with electric clippers, that the horse stands on steel shoes, the clippers are connected to the mains supply and therefore a wet floor could be highly dangerous. I always wear either rubber soled shoes or boots myself; if you can afford it, rubber matting of the solid non-slip variety, is an ideal footing for the horse. However, unless you have several horses to clip, you must make do with the available facilities. Should you have to use the horse's own box, the bed should be lifted and stacked round the walls, leaving only a dry, thin layer on the floor, which has been swept as dry as possible first. A spare box means cleaning up afterwards is simpler, because the horse's own box can be bedded down ready to receive it when it has been clipped. When the horse's own box has been used, all hair must be removed, the bed replaced and the water bucket returned (never have a bucket of water anywhere near electric clippers), all of which takes time. As our garage was next to the loose box, I had a couple of rings in one wall for the horse and a hay net, and the power-point on the wall inside the door. This served as a good grooming/clipping 'box'.

Having decided where to clip, gather together the clippers, blades, oil can, old body brush to clean off the clippers at intervals, soft dandy brush or body brush to remove loose coat as it is clipped from the horse, rugs and blanket, tail bandage, and a good halter – the less metal on the horse the better, but an ordinary headcollar sometimes has to be used. A twitch should also be handy and, unless you know the horse to be quite quiet, a second person to hold the horse. A young horse must have two people to start with. If you are not sure of its behaviour, or you are clipping a difficult horse, take the sensible precaution of wearing a hard hat with chin harness fastened. If possible protect your feet too.

The horse, which should be dry, well groomed and free from all mud and sweat marks, can now be tied up – not too short, but short enough to keep it where you want it. The rope should be tied to a piece of string passed through the ring – should there be an accident, the horse can be cut free swiftly.

I find it a help to plait the mane into straight plaits for a hunter or full clip. This will let you get at the horse's neck without too much risk of removing a section, and ending up as an acquaintance of mine did some years ago, with a forelock but no mane on her best show pony! In any event, manes and forelocks are at risk, should a horse move when the clippers are in that region, so special care must be exercised to avoid accidentally clipping into the mane or forelock. The tail too, should be protected, unless you have a helper to hold it well out of the way when clipping the hindquarters. I plait the end and bandage the top part normally, folding the end of the plait under the bandage, about halfway down. This safeguards the top of the tail and the full part at the end. When the job is finished, the plaits should be taken out and the tail undone.

Should the horse have been clipped before, or if it is cold, place a folded blanket over the horse's loins and quarters to prevent chilling. Move the blanket around as necessary.

If your horse has never been clipped before, do accustom it beforehand to the noise of running clippers. This may take a day or two, depending on the horse. Before clipping River

Gipsy as a four-year-old for the first time, I plugged the clippers into the socket in the garage and let them run while she was tied up with her hay net after being groomed. At first the clippers were well away from her, but then I brought them closer — clippers in one hand and a reward in the other. She was very interested and even touched the running clippers with her nose. I laid the blades flat on her neck to let her feel the sensation, rewarding her at the same time. She then permitted me to trim under her chin. Two days later she was chaser clipped — one of the easiest horses I have ever had to do.

Once the horse is ready, plug in the clippers, if electric, preferably to a three-pin socket (light sockets are not to be encouraged), the plug fused with a 3-amp fuse (2 amp in some cases). Strictly speaking clippers are designed to be used without an earthed plug, but it is far safer to use one, though no wire is connected to the earth with double-insulated clippers. Standing well back from the horse, switch on and let the clippers run. Listen for the hum of the motor and if it is running smoothly, adjust the tension screw — turn down tight, and back, somewhere between half a turn and a turn-and-a-half, according to the make and model of the machine. Oil the blades and the oil holes, remembering to repeat the process at frequent intervals during the 2 to 2½ hours that it will take to clip the horse.

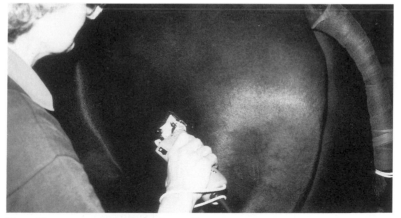

River Gipsy 13 years 9 months. Lister Showman clipper; note how neatly it fits into the hand, and the safety loop round the wrist. The tail is bandaged and plaited for safety. Finishing touches to a clip using fine blades.

The time has now come to start clipping. Approach the horse quietly, talking to it to reassure it. Clippers can be used in either hand, but do place the safety strap over your wrist – this prevents you from dropping them accidentally. Before placing the blades on the horse, test them on your own hand: they should not be hot, and on no account should you feel a shock. If in any doubt switch off immediately and disconnect the plug. If the clippers are running correctly, proceed with the hindquarters or lower half of the body, well away from the head.

The secret of good clipping is to let the clipper blades glide into the coat in the direction that the coat grows, keeping the points of the blades in a slight upwards curve to let them glide smoothly over the skin. Never force the blades into the coat. Do shorter parts rather than trying to cover too long a section if the coat is very dense. Forcing the blades into the coat only clogs and blunts them, causing them to pull at and hurt the horse. Once this has happened you will have an unwilling partner – and who can blame the horse.

To achieve the desired result, certain points must be observed for the five different clips we identified earlier.

Full

This is the easiest clip in some respects as there are only two sections to mark out, the rest comes off. At the root of the tail an area in the shape of an inverted 'V' must be left. This is an equal-sided triangle. Clip slightly wide of the final lines and then very carefully run the clippers up from the root of the tail to a point directly at the centre of the horse's back, and then repeat on the other side; you should be left with a neat 'V'. The mane is the only other area which needs a very steady hand. Here, again, a run below the final line is necessary. The horse's head will need to be turned away slightly to stretch the skin along the mane line on the side that is being clipped. *Make sure you do not clip into the mane.* Before clipping examine carefully how low the mane grows, as they vary, by pulling a small section outwards and clip just below the roots along the crest of the mane. It is easiest to clip the near side and then the off – here the mane must be lifted and most likely the clippers held in the left hand.

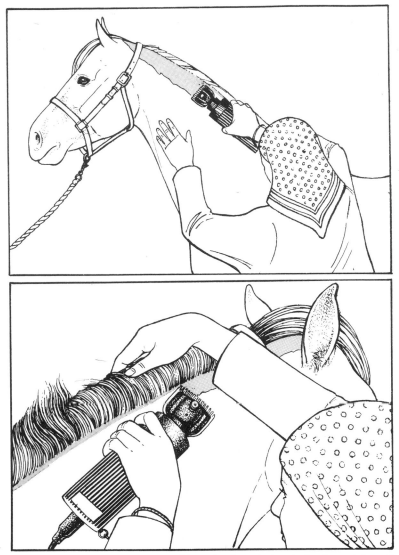

Clipping the neck requires care. Keep the horse's head steady and turn it away from the clippers to keep the skin taut. Run the clippers up the neck taking care to avoid the base of the mane. Unruly manes should be put in plaits or bunches to keep them clear of the clippers.

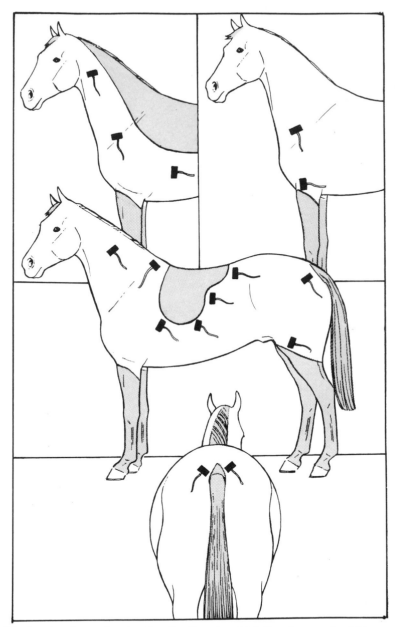

The hunter clip — showing the directions in which the clippers should be used

Hunter

This clip is similar to the full, but the legs must be carefully marked out. The line on the legs slopes to the rear. The forelegs come back to form a neat pointed-shaped 'V' at the elbows whereas the hind legs have their 'V' a hand's width above the hock at the rear and just below the stifle in the front. Do ensure that the 'V's are even: they should be at the same height on both legs (use your hand — it is the best measure when clipping). The inside of the leg is clipped as well as the outside.

The saddle patch is achieved by placing the horse's own saddle on its back and clipping round it. Here, again, clip wide of the eventual finished saddle path to allow for an even finish. Some people mark out the patch with chalk, or you can run your finger round the saddle against the hair to give the outline. Be prepared to take both time and trouble over achieving a neat patch or the horse will look awful when the saddle is off. Having cut the rough outline, work carefully inwards until the edge of the saddle is reached on both sides, with about 13 mm (½ in.) to spare. Now comes the tricky part — trimming the edges. With very short, gentle bursts, pass the clipper blades under the very outside edge and lift through the hair to cut it off square. Repeat this all the way round till the patch is neat and tidy. If you have never clipped a patch before, do not clip right in to the saddle, but practise 'edging' on the part still to be removed. Once you have the hang of it, clip to the saddle and finish off the patch properly. But do make certain before starting to clip that the saddle is in the correct place on the horse's back as nothing looks worse than a patch with the saddle sitting in a completely different place. Remember too, to follow the outline of the saddle over the horse's withers, ensuring that both sides meet bang central over the spine. The 'V' for the root of the tail is the same as for a full clip.

Blanket

Here, again, you will need the horse's own saddle. Clip round the front half following the outline of the flaps back as far as

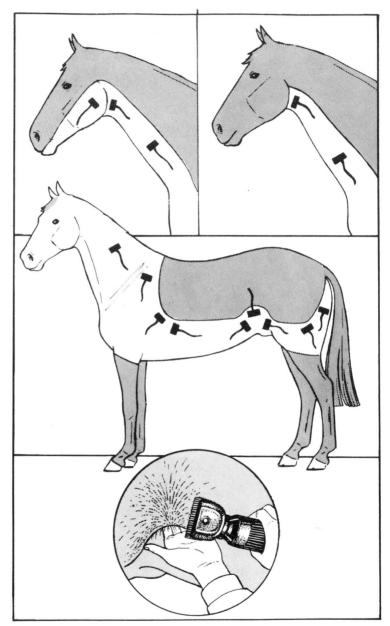

Showing the directions in which the clippers should be used: top (left and right), trace clip; centre and bottom, blanket clip.

the girth, allowing approximately 2.5 cm (1 in.) to spare. Everything in front of the line (head, neck and chest), is then clipped as for a full or hunter clip. The legs, too, are marked out as for a hunter clip, but the whole of the back is left up to the rear of the saddle. Some people like to cut straight round to the tail. I do not: it is extremely ugly and leaves the coat on the area which sweats most. If you work a horse with a coat on you will notice that it sweats most on the flanks and up the hindquarters to the root of the tail. This is why you should clip a neat half-circle over each flank; the size depends on how hard you are going to work the horse, but roughly to within 15 cm (6 in.) of the top of the natural whirl. You should also remove the coat up either side of the hindquarters, here again rounding off the corners for smartness and to clear the sweat area. Clipping the half-circle over the flanks requires the clippers to be used in both directions — follow the line of the hair. Rounding the corners over the quarters calls for short runs as adopted in clipping the saddle patch. Again, use your hand as a measure and ensure that both sides are even when viewed not only from either side, but from the front and, above all, the rear.

Chaser

Clip the body behind the saddle as for a blanket clip, but do not follow the saddle round over the shoulders. From the bottom of the saddle flap, curve the line upwards across the shoulder to the neck and then run in a dead straight line up the side of the neck to terminate on the edge of the mane where the bridle slot has been removed behind the ears. Some people come up lower and then turn upwards to the mane, leaving slightly more coat on the neck. Either is correct, but I have over the years come to favour the former for smartness, and I think it is easier. The head, lower neck and chest are clipped as in the other clips.

Trace

HIGH This clip is similar to a chaser, but the neck is taken lower to a point just above the windpipe, behind the jawbone. The underside of the jaw up to the windpipe is also clipped,

35

and the face to the edge of the bridle cheek is sometimes included as well. The rest of the head is left unclipped.

MEDIUM The whole line of the clip is dropped down by about 10 cm (4 in.) and on the head only the underside of the jaw is taken out. This is the normal trace clip.

LOW The hindquarters are not clipped or perhaps only a very narrow strip the width of the clipper-head is taken out across the hind legs with the body left unclipped except for right underneath the belly, the chest, the windpipe and the underside of the jaw. This clip is only used for horses and ponies turned out in a New Zealand rug.

No matter which of the various clips you decide to adopt, the following rules will apply. Do not force the clipper blades into the coat. Stop clipping at frequent intervals and test to ensure that the clippers are not overheating (some do run hot and must be cooled off) and to remove the loose hair from the blades with a soft brush (an old body or water brush works very well). Reoil and switch on again to resume clipping. While the clippers are cooling, brush over the area clipped and look for areas you may have missed.

Clean the clippers frequently during clipping and brush off the hair. Lister Showman.

Oil along the blades while the clippers are running and oil both ends. Lister Showman.

Put oil into the holes on top to oil the inside works. Lister Showman.

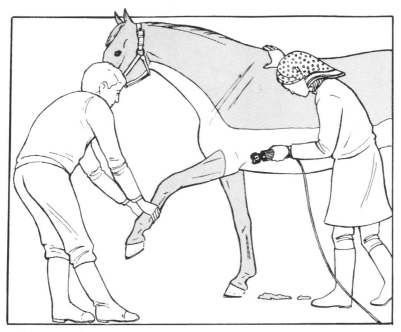

Holding a leg forward to stretch the skin to facilitate the clipping of the foreleg.

When clipping the forelegs on the inside it helps to have someone to hold up a leg to enable the skin to be stretched; if no help is available, you should hold the leg forward and clip with the other hand. When clipping heads start at the muzzle and work very gently upwards. Take very great care not to damage the eyes and do the ears last. Many horses hate their heads being clipped and you must go very slowly. If restraint is necessary, then a twitch on the nose (never the ear) is often kinder than fighting to work without one, but some horses are equally frightened of a twitch, never force the twitch on these horses; patience must prevail. Before clipping the head, brush the horse over and rug up warmly. If they are warm, horses will often stand more willingly than if cold. Remember, their warm coats have just been removed and if they are left unrugged they could contract a chill.

Legs, too, if they are being clipped, require time. Remove the hair from the hock or knee upwards first as this is easy.

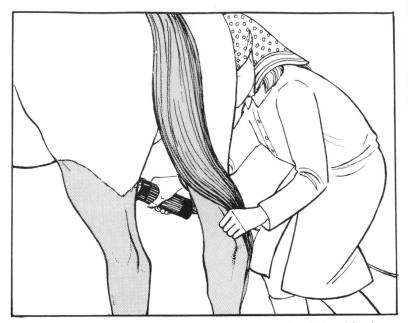

Clipping a hind leg from the opposite side with the free hand placed firmly on the hock

Then move down to the coronet and start clipping upwards. Work carefully and thoroughly round each leg in turn following the lie of the hair, being careful of the ergots (small horny growths behind the fetlock joint) and chestnuts (found above the knee and just below the hocks on the insides of the legs). Look out for the change of hair direction in the centre of the belly when clipping in that area, and for any hernia. Many horses have small ones and care must be exercised not to clip against them. Watch out too for a mare's udder and teats and a gelding's sheath. Some horses do not like being clipped between their hind legs, so place a hand firmly on the hock, before bending underneath. It is sometimes easier to clip across under a horse than to do the inside of the leg on the side at which you are standing.

Having satisfied yourself that the job has been done neatly and thoroughly, switch off and disconnect the clippers, removing them to a safe place to cool and await thorough cleaning. Next, sweep up all the loose hair from the floor (at intervals during clipping you should have swept up the hair into a corner to avoid slipping). This hair will stink if burnt and it will not rot if left on the muck heap, so pick it up and stuff it into an old paper sack and put it out with the household refuse.

We have so far dealt with clipping a horse in work or for work. It is also sometimes necessary to clip certain areas prior to surgery. Fine blades are required for this type of clipping as the coat must be removed as close to the skin as possible.

In the case of an owner having to clear the coat from around an injury, it is essential to clip the hair well back from any cut if it is going to heal satisfactorily and with the minimum of scarring. Hand clippers are probably the best, unless you know your horse will accept the vibrations of electric clippers. Having clipped well back to leave the surrounding area easy to clean, then, using scissors very gently, take the hair as close as possible, being careful not to fill the wound with hair. You will be amazed at how well even serious wounds will heal once clipped clear of hair − I have seen this proved time and again. The replacement hair too, seems to grow in the correct colour much more easily. The scabs which form on a wound, due to pus oozing from it, can be bathed off if the skin is not covered in matted hair. If the hair is left, it will hold infection around the wound, and very often increase the size of the area, resulting in an ugly scar, that never need have been, had the area been clipped at the outset.

So much for horses that are willing to be clipped, but some horses are a problem to clip; they range from the restive through those that are very ticklish or frightened, to those that will not have clippers near them at any price. Now these, in the interest of safety to both the person doing the clipping and the horse, need special care. A twitch − either the old-fashioned cord type or the new metal ones, will often suffice. To use a twitch satisfactorily the horse requires an upper lip which will permit the twitch to fit behind the front of the muzzle, thereby preventing the twitch slipping straight off again which happens with a dainty-muzzled horse. Some horses hate a twitch, and this only makes matters worse. River Gipsy, though

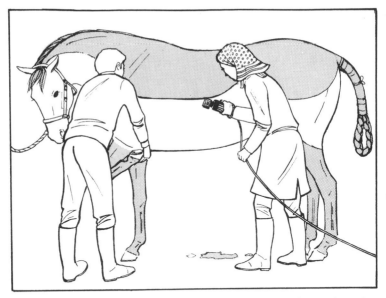

Holding a foreleg up to help control the horse while it is being clipped

A twitch applied to the upper lip is another means of control for horses that are a problem to clip

willing to accept a twitch when young, will not now tolerate one, because, sadly, someone in my absence was once very severe, leaving a deep cut in her upper lip. Though so good to clip as a youngster, she now, owing to over 180 gunshot pellets working back out of her body over the years, is too ticklish and apprehensive to accept the clippers without being doped first. Some people despise doping, but I prefer a calm horse to being kicked. It is far safer for all concerned. I am fortunate; the drug A.C.P. will work on River Gipsy, and, because I am experienced, is one I am permitted to inject into the muscle myself. *No owner* should inject their horse themselves unless their vet is absolutely satisfied that they are capable. If not the vet must give the injection, using whichever drug is deemed most suitable for the horse in question. There are a variety available now and your vet will decide. If you are permitted to give A.C.P. yourself, you have to collect it from your vet who will put the required dose in a syringe complete with needle.

The size of the dose depends on the horse and how restive it is. In warm weather I have found River Gipsy's present dose takes about 24−48 hours to wear off completely, whereas in cold weather it tends to wear off almost before the clipping is finished, leaving her as bright as a button the next day. I give the A.C.P. injection into the hindquarters, and it takes about 20 minutes to take, but the horse may fight it. Your vet will advise you on the length of time required before starting to clip. If you know your horse will not react adversely, then it is safe to stay in the box with it, otherwise give the injection and get out of the box until you are sure it is not going to go berserk while the drug takes. Mercifully I have never had this happen, but I have heard of some pretty frightening cases, so be sensible. River Gipsy merely gets sleepy and goes on eating her hay. (A horse should have a full net of the best hay available to take its mind off the clipping.) Once satisfied the horse is ready to clip, clip quickly and calmly; do not rush, but do not waste time fiddling, you can tidy up at the end if the horse is still relaxed and willing.

River Gipsy, will, provided I do not try to hang onto her head, let me clip her single-handed, using Lister Showman low-volt clippers. I do her hindquarters first and then her belly, followed by the rest of her body, neck and finally the

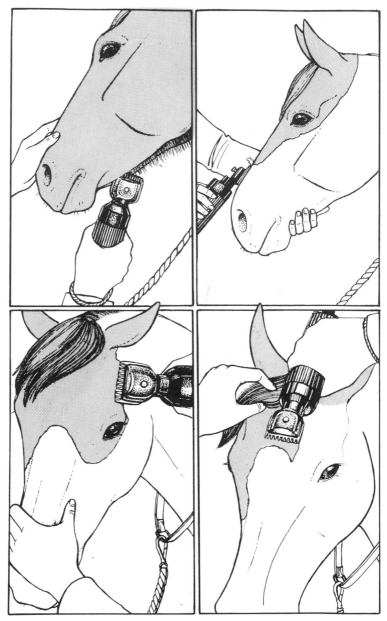

Clipping the head

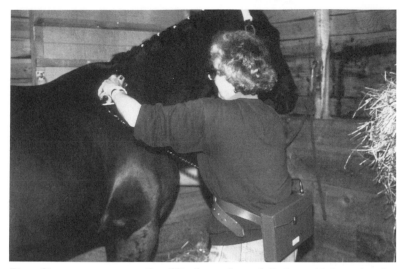

River Gipsy 13 years 9 months. Clip the neck carefully to avoid damaging the mane. Lister's Showman clipper.

head. If she is relaxed she will even let me do her ears, but it requires great patience.

When clipping the neck and head, I clip as far up the neck as I can on both sides, including the windpipe — following the twirls of hair to ensure the clip is close — then I do those parts of the head I can with the headcollar on if the horse is restive; with a horse who enjoys being clipped, I remove the headcollar at the start and fasten it round its neck. An adjustable headcollar is a great help, because the noseband can be undone and done up again as required. I like to start at the nose (though I leave the whiskers to last as they can be done later if necessary) and work up the bridge of the nose then under the jaw and round the cheeks and fat parts of the face; I then clip across the forehead, taking great care not to get too close to the eyes or remove the forelock. The important thing is to ensure you follow the lie of the hair.

Lastly I clip the ears. I work first one side then the other; moving to and fro with horses who are nervous about having their ears handled. I find it a help to grasp the mane firmly just where the poll section has been removed, hold it for a few minutes and then clip; it often has a calming effect. Similarly,

43

holding the forelock helps. Hold the ear gently and clip from tip to base across the back and then fold the sides of the ear together and clip down the front, or place the hand across the back of the ear and press down gently to open the ear on the inside and clip the inside, this method stops the hair falling back in to the ear which is essential. Some horses prefer the near ear clipped from the off side.

With horses who enjoy having their heads done, I can clip one side completely and then clip the other side, oiling the clippers frequently to keep them clean and cool. Work with short sweeps, being very careful of protruding bones, eyes etc.

Should you, by any misfortune, knock the top of an eye, you may well bruise it; if you have, a shadow will appear about 48 hours later near where the eye was hit. In some cases it may take longer for the bruise to appear, but, over the ensuing weeks, it will traverse the eye. In time, with care and treatment, it will go, and the eye will regain its normal brightness. It is, however, essential to nurse the problem carefully. Ensure that the horse has a clean, dry bed so that, when it lies down at night, the eye is free from fumes emitted from a damp, deep-litter bed, and keep it away from draughts; both these factors prolong the trouble. Eye ointment will probably also be required; do apply it exactly as directed by the veterinary surgeon and complete the treatment.

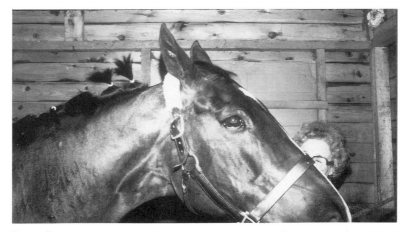

River Gipsy 13 years 9 months. Note warts in ear; Clip areas such as these with great care

Accidents will happen; a bang during clipping over the eye will lead to a bruise that can take up to 6 months or so to clear.

Do not rush the clipping of the head; be patient, but firm, coaxing and encouraging as you go. Should your horse really hate it, then you may, like many more grooms and owners nowadays, opt for leaving the head unclipped. This is safer and in some cases the only answer, particularly if, even when doped, the horse will still not accept the clippers. It is not worth having an accident. Do try, though, to clip to a given point on both sides of the head and finish with a neat line. Decide first how far to go, and then stop so that the area is not all ragged lines and steps.

Not clipping the head can prove to be a problem with horses in fast work because when they sweat the heads get damp and sticky, and they may get restless and cross. For this reason I like to clip if I can.

The Wolseley prototype trimmer (the Skylark) I have been trying out will, I think, solve many problems for the owners of horses that, like Gipsy, hate having their ears and heads clipped. Gipsy has let me trim the inside of her ears with these trimmers, without being doped, and was content to let them glide all over her head. I am longing for the finished article to be on the market.

Remember: when you have given your own injection, you have the responsibility of disposing of the syringe and needle safely. Put the needle back into its cover and place both into a sealed container if possible − a tin with a tight lid will do − and then place in the refuse bag. *Never* throw needles away uncovered, or in a place where they could be found by children or someone wishing to use them for illegal purposes. *All drugs are dangerous and must be treated with care and kept out of reach of children and other animals.*

6 Care of the Clipped Horse

Care of the clipped horse is extremely important for it has been robbed of all its natural protection and warmth and thus has no means of combating either the elements or changes in temperature. Rugs and blankets that are clean and really warm replace the horse's natural coat in the stables, and during exercise if the weather is not fine and mild.

Before clipping the horse, it is as well to have had at least a night rug on the horse overnight and probably during daytime too. This not only helps get the coat in a better condition for clipping, but also prepares the horse to carry rugs once its natural coat has been removed. A warm, thick blanket is therefore required to go under the night rug for additional warmth. A slightly thinner rug and blanket can be used if the clipping is done early in the autumn or late summer. The horse must be really warm, but not overcome by heat. There are various types of rug on the market, but I have dealt in detail with these in my book *Horse By Horse — A Guide to Equine Care*. Let it therefore suffice to say buy only top quality rugs that fit both round the collar (neck) and by the tail, and are of such a length as to cover the sides of the horse and wrap under the girth without causing wrinkles behind the elbows. Remember, the horse will spend many hours in rugs and if they do not fit properly they will rub, causing discomfort. Until recently I had a strong preference for wool or jute, natural fibres rather than man-made ones and especially for use in frosty weather, but nowadays jute rugs of real quality and cut are extremely hard to obtain. Present day jute rugs used as spring and autumn rugs are still feasible, though with the vast improvement in nylon rugs and their linings, even I have been converted to the modern rug, *provided* they are either cotton or fleece lined to prevent static electricity. Nylon in particular has a tendency to create static electricity which some horses dislike, but a woollen blanket placed under the nylon rug will often solve this problem. However, in very cold weather, nylon rugs may become stiff and crackle which many horses will not accept. A well-cut cotton summer sheet, padded at the withers, and placed under the rug, and/or blanket, also helps to prevent static electricity, especially on a fully clipped horse. In addition a blanket on top of a sheet does not slip so easily.

The original nylon rug linings were also nylon — some still are — and these I would not buy, but those with cotton linings are very soft, cosy and kind to the skin. Fleece is also soft and cosy, and although excellent for New Zealand and exercise rugs, it has one major drawback in the stable; it attracts shavings if they are used for bedding. Once embedded in the fleece they are very hard to remove, and, if left, they can cause skin problems and itching. So use a rug lining suitable for your horse's bedding.

Modern rugs come in many styles of cut and fastening; some excellent, some good, some passable, but others are a pure waste of money. Choose your rug with great care. It must fit correctly all over, allowing room for the horse to get up and down safely without hindrance, and it must be comfortable. If the rug is too deep there is a real risk that the horse will be hampered getting up; if it is too shallow the horse's tummy will not be protected. If the rug is too short the horse will get chilled, and if too long it will drag back causing pressure along the spine by hanging down over the tail. Many people go in for very long rugs hoping to keep their horse warmer, but it is far better to have a rug tailored to fit snuggly round the quarters. A well-fitting rug should reach the root of the tail and come to the front of the withers, in order to fit snuggly round the shoulders, so that it does not drag back or restrict the windpipe when the horse is grazing or eating off the ground.

Modern rugs come in several thicknesses; very thick for cold weather, medium for normal weather, and lightweight for warmer weather. This is all very well but you must then have a series of rugs to regulate the warmth according to the weather, which could prove expensive. With the temperature varying during the day, you cannot adjust the rug to the temperature without changing it; whereas with two or three rugs, or a rug and blanket, you can remove one for as long as necessary and then replace it.

The warmth and thickness of a rug depends on what the filling is made of; plain blanketing, a padding of some kind that is quilted to varying thicknesses, or a reflective material which reflects the horse's own body heat back onto its body thereby keeping it warm. New fillings are coming on the market all the time, so study them carefully and choose the one best suited to your horse's needs.

If you do choose to use only one rug, it is essential to have a spare blanket handy to place over the horse's quarters while saddling up in cold weather and for grooming, otherwise a clipped horse will get chilled. I still prefer to use a combination of two or three rugs and blankets that are warm but light. For the last few winters, since moving to East Anglia, I have been forced to use up to four or more to keep River Gipsy warm enough in open barn boxes, because she feels the cold. The type of stabling is a prime factor in the number of rugs required, the more enclosed the box (which should be well ventilated but completely draught free) the fewer rugs are required. I am now experimenting with a duvet; I have added extra lines of quilting stitches to firm the filling and have cut the neck to fit snuggly round her shoulders and across her chest, and it is fastened by a proper strap and buckle. The duvet is placed over her blanket and under a thin brushed-nylon rug with her flectron-filled Thermalite rug on top. The summer sheet is still worn underneath her blanket to prevent it slipping. In due course, once I am sure the duvet will not slip, it could be used in place of the summer sheet, because it is cotton both sides and 'breathes'. The one drawback is that single-bed sized duvets are only 1.4 m (4 ft. 6 in.) wide, making them rather shallow, however, they are the perfect length − 1.9 m (6 ft. 6 in.) − from which to shape the neck. Large horses would require a double-bed sized duvet.

I prefer a well-fitting roller to fasten rugs. Jute rollers wear out far too fast, so now I have a made to measure navy-blue union-web roller, to ensure the pad fits correctly and holds the

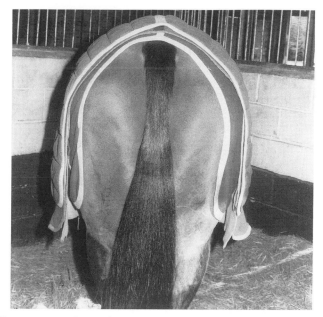

River Gipsy 12 years 8 months in an open barn with cage boxes, requires several layers of rugs and blankets to combat the cold. Here she wears a summer sheet, a blanket, an old day rug, and they are topped by a Thermalite nylon rug. Rugs must be put on carefully and evenly.

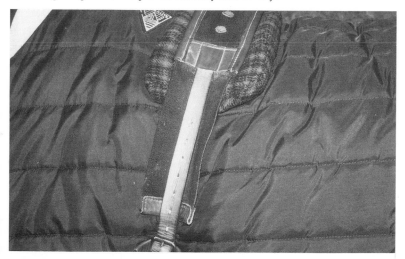

A four-inch single rawhide strap, union-web roller over a shaped foam pad in a tweed cover.

rugs without pinching; it also matches Gipsy's rug which looks smart. I find that a properly made and correctly fitting roller secures the rugs best because it prevents them sliding back and pulling on the chest and windpipe. Under the roller I use a foam pad shaped to fit with a channel cut in the underside to match that on the roller (5 cm [2 in.] foam will bear 2.5 cm [1 in.] being cut out), and then the ends are tapered on the underside to allow the sides to conform to the horse's sides and ensure a smooth fit. The pad prevents the roller from pinching the horse, and also allows him to breathe freely, because the foam gives with the horse's respiratory movements.

Most people prefer crossed surcingles; these are attached to the rug and cross under the horse's belly. They are fine if they stay fastened, but many do not; they unhook themselves, leaving the rug free to slip off. If only one rug is used then crossed surcingles are acceptable because they remove pressure from the spine. However, two or more rugs with crossed surcingles mean that the horse has a series of straps passing and crossing under its belly which could rub or pinch. Sometimes a roller is used as well, strapping the horse up like a parcel! Remember, no two horses are the same shape and fixed straps therefore never cross in the same place on every horse, so the fit varies. The fit of the rug neck plays an important part in the positioning of fixed staps; if it is too large the rug slips back taking the straps with it and placing them far too far back, rather like a bucking strap on a rodeo saddle. The tension on the straps is important as well; if they are too loose there is a risk that the horse could get a hoof caught in them when it gets up, so do ensure the straps fit snuggly without being too tight.

Leg straps round all four legs in place of a roller or crossed surcingles, have been used on some rugs. These, if the rug fits well, have their uses when a horse repeatedly removes its rugs fastened by other means. Some will get their rugs off regardless, the only answer is to try very hard to find a fastening that is not only effective but safe. Hind leg straps in these cases do help, but they must fit and not hang down below the hock.

Horses require rugs and blankets after clipping. Two are normal, but three, or perhaps more depending on the horse, are essential in bitterly cold weather. Most horses will not worry at a low temperature of around 20°F (−7°C), but when the reading plummets much below that owners must ensure that their horses are kept warm. Extra rugs are essential. A word of warning: do not hurry to remove these extra rugs if the weather is changeable, or if there has been much snow. The first fall of snow and hard weather most horses will take in their stride under normal circumstances, but a second spell will leave everything colder and the thaw can chill very seriously. If the horse is hunter clipped, then bandages may be necessary too, and certainly with a full clip.

The freshly clipped horse − either after the first clip or another later in the season − must be given a quick, but thorough brush over to stimulate the skin, clean off loose grease and hair, and generally make it comfortable. Keep a rug on while doing this. Then rerug: shake the blanket thoroughly, place it on the horse, then shake the rug and put this on top. If a third rug is used, place the jute rug on the top with the woollen blankets and rugs underneath; if a quilted nylon rug is used as the third rug, place it over the jute because it will either slip, or it will cause the other rugs to do so. Fasten the rugs in place using a roller with a pad underneath to protect the spine from pressure. Now wipe out the horse's eyes, nose and under the tail − using a separate sponge for each − with warm water to make the horse comfortable and remove any loose hair that could irritate it. Remove all plaits and brush out the mane and tail well − any curls will come out very quickly, especially if a water brush is passed lightly over the mane to lay it.

If bandages are required, apply these now over gamgee or felt foam − stockinette can be used, but wool are best. Remember to fasten the tapes on the outside and knot, before turning the knot under for safety. Though many bandages still have tapes, velcro has taken over to a large extent, and far better in most cases. There are no knots to get in the way, and it is quick to fasten and unfasten, providing the horse does not object to the ripping sound. Ensure velcro straps are long enough to pass round the leg to give a good grip and that the rough part is kept free of fluff so that they fasten strongly. The straps are either one or two inches wide. When rolling velcro-fastened bandages fold the gripping part of velcro back onto itself, this keeps it clean; just pull it apart once the bandage is on and press firmly to the soft section.

If you have clipped in some place other than the horse's own box, the horse can now be returned to its box which should have a really deep bed between 10−15 cm (4−6 in.) when compressed, and right up to every wall however big the box. The bedding should also be banked up the walls at least 30 cm (12 in.) for added warmth and protection. A skimped bed is a false economy. Keep the horse warm and his food intake will be more efficiently used than if he is cold and using food to maintain body temperature. If you have had to clip in the horse's own box, then a good clean, dry bed must be laid on the freshly swept floor. The clipped coat must be cleaned away before rebedding the box.

So much for the initial care of a clipped horse. Each day it must be thoroughly groomed, quartered (lightly brushed over) and rerugged first thing in the morning, strapped thoroughly on return from, or as soon as convenient after, exercise. If possible, it is best to do this while the pores of the horse's skin are open, but if time does not permit then rerug on return and groom later. Should the horse be hot on his return, fold up the front of the rug for a short time to allow the horse to cool off, but do not leave for too long. At evening stables the rugs should be removed and replaced again. If two rugs are used and you therefore have two breast straps, they must fit perfectly, one over the other allowing room for the horse to lower its head to reach the floor, but not so much that the rug hangs off in front. When all the rugs and the roller are in place run your hand down under the roller on each side to remove any wrinkles and ease the roller into the most comfortable position for the horse. Now go to the back and gently tug each rug in turn, starting with the one next to the horse, to remove all ridges. The centre seams of the rugs should match the horse's spine. It is a great help to mark the centre of a blanket back and front, thus saving time when trying to get it square.

While exercising in normal weather, say up to December, the horse should not need a rug under the saddle, but on wet days and once the weather turns cold a rug is essential. In bitter weather two rugs, or a rug and a blanket, are required. Some people are so unthinking that while they pile sweaters and coats on themselves they remove all the rugs from their horses', often freshly clipped, backs and set forth in freezing temperatures. It is little wonder that these horses suffer in the end. Whereas hunting or fast work will keep a horse warm, exercising with walking and slow trotting will not.

Exercise rugs vary; in fine weather, the blanket-type or rugging is suitable, but in wet weather waterproof rugs are necessary. As rugs are expensive, and normal waterproof rugs on their own are cold unless lined or placed over a rug or blanket, I have designed and had made by Thermalite a cordura rug lined with thermal fleece. This stops static electricity in frosty conditions, and keeps a clipped horse warm in wind and rain as well as frost, but with very little sweating, because the rug 'breathes'. The rug has a shaped front, so that I do not need to turn the front up under the saddle flaps, the girth passes through loops to prevent it slipping back, and the rug is shaped over the withers to allow the horse to lift its. head without causing pressure on the withers or spine. Choose a rug that fits well because an ill-fitting one will rub, and use a fillet string to anchor the back of the rug in wind. The soft, thermal fleece also does away with the need for a separate numnah.

Many horses these days are kept part in and part out of the stable, being trace, blanket or chaser clipped, to enable their owners to ride at weekends and work during the week. This is perfectly acceptable if the horse has shelter in the field, is well fed and has a really warm New Zealand rug that fits. The rug must be warm *and* waterproof — many are not — and cover the horse to protect it from the elements without hampering it. I *do not* approve of those owners who make their horses sleep out in rugs once they have been clipped, or those callous types, occasionally encountered, who buy a trace-clipped horse and strip it of all covering in bitter weather as they cannot be bothered to rug it. Such people should never own a horse. Some owners even make their horses sleep in New Zealand rugs which are hard and rub. Think of your horse's comfort and put fresh dry rugs on it at night. With a New Zealand rug, ensure that the surcingle does not press on the spine, the leg straps fit and the breast strap or straps hold the neck of the rug in the correct position. If a surcingle is used, stitch a pad of foam, covered in material, on the underside to form a soft roller over the back, in order to prevent damage from pressure on the spine or from rolling. Fixed surcingles seldom fit safely, far better to have a loose one that can be placed in the correct position.

Nowadays, the variety of New Zealand rugs on the market is ever-growing. Some have straps on all four legs only which is fine if the rug fits, otherwise the straps must be moved so that they do fit the horse, or they will pull and rub. Others have straps running from the front to the hind legs. Both these types of rug require no form of surcingle and are self-righting when the horse rolls, or said to be. Ordinary surcingles tend to leave the rug where it finished up after the roll which is not satisfactory as the horse's stomach can get chilled. The ones that have impressed me most are those with hind leg straps and crossed surcingles. This system prevents pressure on the spine, the sides cannot flap in the wind, and they really seem to stay in place.

Many New Zealands are still made of various grades of canvas; the good ones are still very good, but many are of poor quality. If you choose canvas do save up and get the best you can, particularly if the horse has to use it on a daily basis. Heavy-grade nylon that is resistant to damage under normal use is proving very satisfactory, it is much lighter than canvas, and dries well, but must be well lined. If a nylon rug does not have its own warm lining then do place another stable rug under the New Zealand in cold weather. Linings can be blanketing, quilting, (cotton is best), and thermal fleece, some of which is on the thin side and some of a good deep pile. Blanketing is fine in spring and autumn with moderate weather, but not suitable for severe weather as it lacks insulation and warmth. Thermal fleece seems satisfactory on both counts in my experience with my exercise rug over the last three winters, so much so that I have just bought a new New Zealand rug of storm-proof qualities, with a very soft, deep fleece thermal pile, hind leg straps, crossed surcingles and a strong nylon outer cover with a tail flap to protect the hindquarters from rain and wind. Its fit is excellent. Similar to this rug is another of storm-quality but lined with a quilted lining; this type has no waterproof skirt like the fleece one, so it tends to get rather damp at the bottom in bad weather and the outer

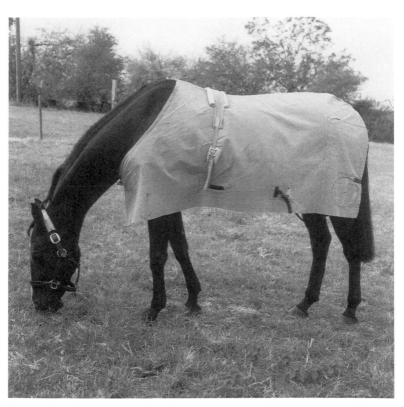

Canvas New Zealand rug with a loose surcingle and hind leg straps. This rug is fine for spring and autumn if the weather is not too cold, but it is not warm enough for cold, damp weather. Note I have padded the withers and buckle of the surcingle to protect River Gipsy when she rolls.

cover rips letting out the quilting, which is something that must be watched and mended quickly to keep out the weather.

One thing I have found with new rugs, is that, in steady rain, the water seeps along the stitching. I have been advised that the stitching should be sealed with a fabric sealer.

7 Trimming and Plaiting

No clipped horse looks correct unless properly trimmed. Unclipped horses also require trimming, unless their breed decrees otherwise. The object of trimming is to enhance the appearance of the horse, aid grooming and generally make the horse feel more comfortable.

Manes, tails, heels and jaws all require trimming from time to time, as do the ergots and chestnuts.

Manes

Manes are trimmed either by pulling, which also thins them, or by hogging. For pulling a horse's mane you need a trimming comb with short teeth fairly close together and a brush to get rid of any tangles. Having brushed the mane thoroughly, comb it through to make it lie straight on the natural side. Some people advocate putting the mane over to the wrong side and then pulling, but I prefer to work from the natural side. Starting at the withers, take a few — and I mean a few — hairs from the ragged ends. Holding them firmly in the fingers of one hand, push the remaining hairs up towards the crest with the comb and then, with a steady, firm pull, remove the hairs that have been singled out. Some manes need a slight jerk to bring out the hairs while others come easily. Work slowly and carefully up the mane towards the poll; when you have completed the first 'run', go back to the start and work up the mane again until the required length has been achieved. Do not pull a mane all in one day if it is thick and long. I will take several sessions. Rush it and the result is a restive horse. At the end of each run, comb and brush the mane straight to

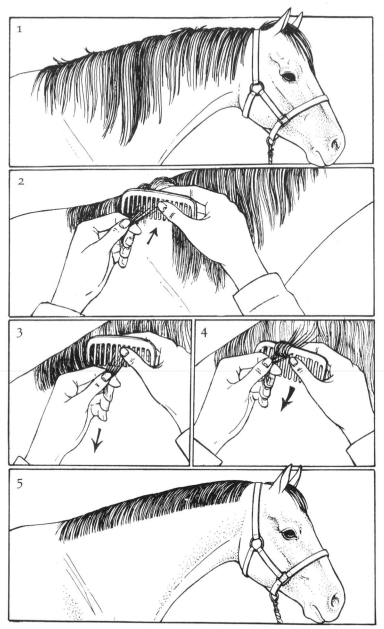

Pulling the mane: 1. An unruly mane, 2. Pushing the shorter hairs back towards the crest, 3. Pulling the long hairs, 4. With a coarse or tough mane it may be necessary to wind the hair round the comb, 5. A neatly pulled mane.

see where the long ends still are. Some sections will require more hair removing than others. Once an even thickness and length have been achieved, tidy up the ends by plucking with your fingers until an overall length of 10−15 cm (4−6 in.) has been reached. Now, reduce the forelock in similar manner to match the mane. Some need only plucking, others require thinning too. Thoroughbred manes require gentler treatment than those of less well-bred horses, as their manes are very fine. Some horses hate having their manes pulled − they can either be twitched (nose only, never an ear), or alternatively, attach a rope to the side of the headcollar nearest to you and hold this in addition to having the horse tied up. Once they find they cannot swing, they often stand, even if unwillingly. With young horses, do go slowly: once they have learnt to accept having their manes pulled, they should be no bother. Hurt them, and you will never have an easy time.

Hogging

Hogging means removing the whole mane with clippers. Standing on the nearside, run the clippers up the centre of the crest from the withers to the poll. Then go round and start at the poll: remove the forelock and clip back down towards the withers. Now run up each side of the crest. Some manes require the clippers to be used from the centre towards the neck in a downward direction as well to round off the crest neatly. Study the lie of the mane and growth direction and clip against it. *Warning* − watch out for short bits of mane flying into your own eyes. A hogged mane on a common horse is tidy and easy to groom, but requires redoing every week to ten days.

Tails

Tails can either be left full or have the top pulled. The latter is achieved by removing a few hairs at a time from either side of the tail and across the top, until only short hairs remain, while the lower end flows out in its natural state. Only pull the tail as far as the broadest part of the horse's hindquarters. Some people go lower, but it is far neater and smarter if not overdone.

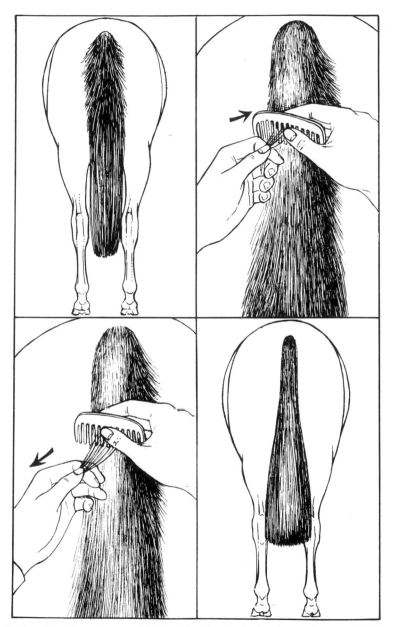

Pulling the tail: 1. A natural tail, 2. Pushing back the shorter hairs, 3. Pulling the long hairs, 4. A neatly pulled tail.

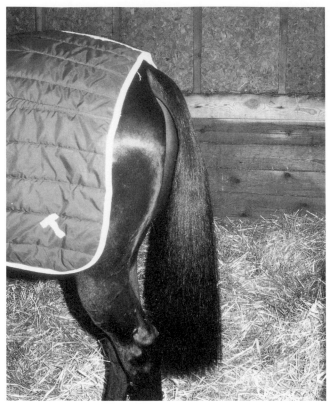

River Gipsy 13 years 10 months. The finished article; a pulled tail.

Pulling a tail from scratch takes time. Never overpull: remove a few hairs each day or every other day, making sure the tail is not becoming sore. Once the tail has been pulled, keeping it tidy takes only a matter of a few minutes either weekly or fortnightly. *Warning* — some horses object very strongly, so go very carefully until you discover if they will agree to having their tails done or not. If not, then get help. There are other ways of pulling but this is my preference.

Heels

Even thoroughbreds with fine hair need their heels trimmed and those with excessive hair will require frequent trimming.

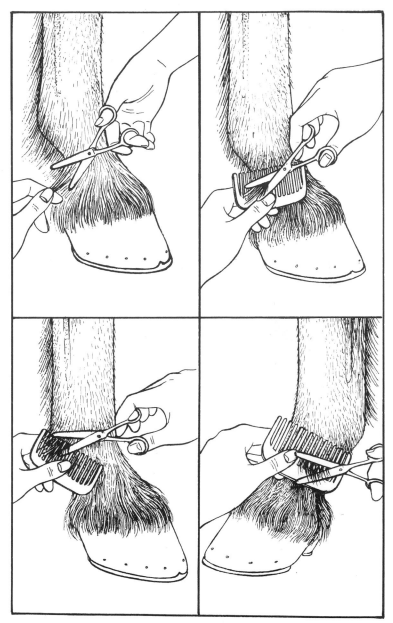

Trimming the hair on the lower leg

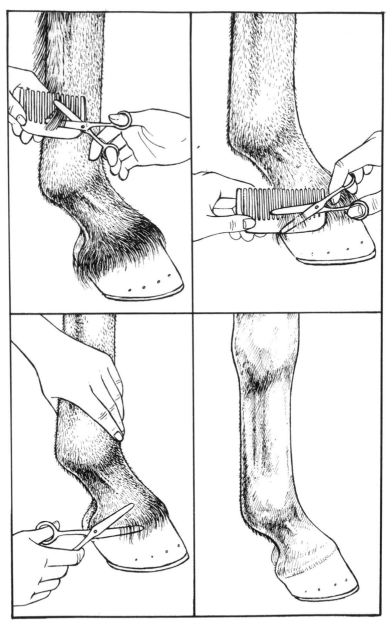

Trimming the hair on the lower leg

Some people never trim the heels, but I have found trimmed heels suffer far less from mud trouble and are much easier to clean than those left untouched. If trouble starts it will be very hard to remove the hair that clogs in the cracks. If the hair is kept short, trouble can be spotted and treated quickly. Trimming is done either with a comb and scissors — using the scissors on top of the comb like a barber — or with clippers — hand clippers are excellent for this job as they do not clip so close. Work from the centre outwards all round the back of the fetlock, tapering into the untouched coat. Some horses require the backs of the tendons and round the front of their coronets trimmed as well. The secret is to start early in the autumn and then it does not show. Electric clippers tend to leave a 'clipped' look, unless coarse blades are used. The Wolseley trimmer has proved an exception, producing an excellent job.

Ergots and Chestnuts

The ergots, situated at the back of the fetlock joint, and the chestnuts, found above the knee on the inside of the forelegs and below the hock on the inside of the hind legs, will require trimming. Both are soft horny growths that should either peel off or, if allowed to become hard, can be pared off with a sharp knife. Take care though that they are not taken too close and bleed. If removed frequently, they come off quite easily.

Jaw

Unsightly whiskers on the horse's jaw not only look ugly, but catch in the bridle making the horse restive. Some people never remove muzzle whiskers but a stabled horse does not need them and is more comfortable without them. The underside of the jaw is trimmed with clippers and if the sides of the face are to be trimmed too, work from the jawbone sideways, tapering out the trim as you reach the cheekbone. In this way, the head can be made to look much smaller. *Never* remove the eye lashes.

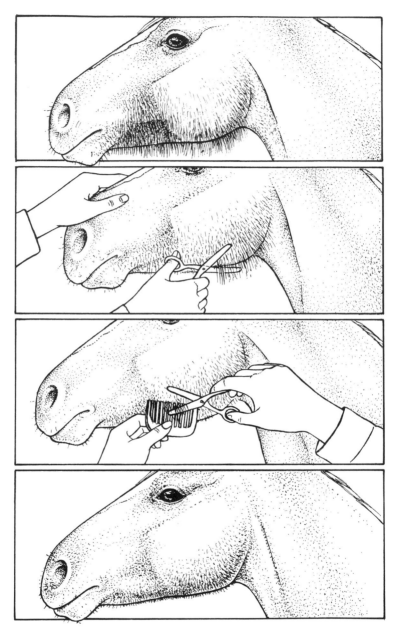

Trimming the whiskers and excess hair on the jaw

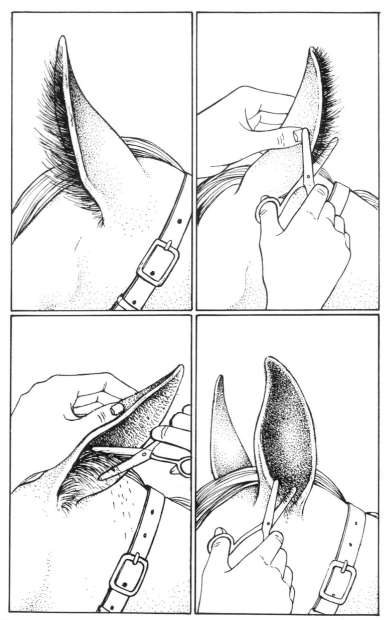

Trimming the hair on the inside of the ears

Ears

The ears should not have all the long hairs inside removed, as these are nature's protection against flies, insects and dust, acting as a filter. Nevertheless, the excess hair may be removed by gently folding the sides of the ear together with one hand, and carefully trimming off the hair beyond the edge of the ear with either clippers or scissors to produce a neat outline.

Plaiting

MANES Nowadays manes seem to have any number of plaits though seven used to be the accepted number. Neck plaits must be of an uneven number with one in the forelock. For plaiting you require a comb, brush, water, elastic bands, needle and strong thread matching the colour of the mane. First, comb and brush the mane straight – having pulled it to about 10–15 cm (4–6 in.) Now, starting at the withers – always start away from the head and work towards it so that the horse has time to get used to the sensation – divide the mane into the number of plaits required, securing each bunch with an elastic band. The first plait will be on the withers if this section of the mane has not been removed. If clipped off, then the first plait will be at the lower end of the neck. Each bundle of hair is dampened with water before being plaited as this helps the hairs to stay in place; some people use hair setting lotion, but I dislike this practice. Take the first bunch and subdivide into three, holding a section between each of your first three fingers. Place a length of thread over the centre section and start to plait firmly by placing first the right hand and then the left hand section over the centre and repeating right, left until the plait is complete to the very end of the hair. Pull the thread gently down until it is within the firm plait and bind the end, knotting as you go. You can either leave the plait straight while you do the others (the choice is yours), or sew up right away. Thread the needle (a strong one) with the end of the thread in the mane and pass the needle up through the plait near the crest to double it. Double the plaits again by passing the needle back down the plait and up once more; the thread is then passed sideways to the right and brought back up, and

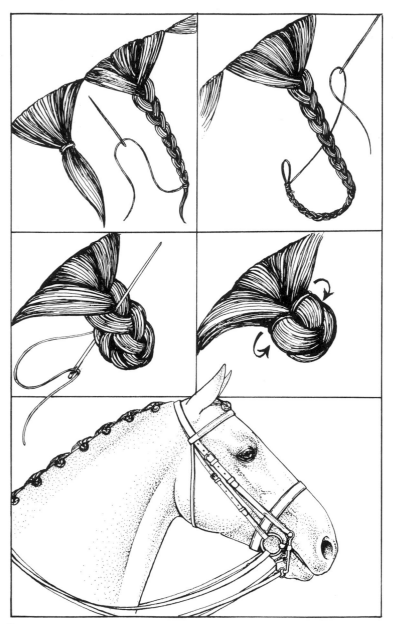

Plaiting the mane

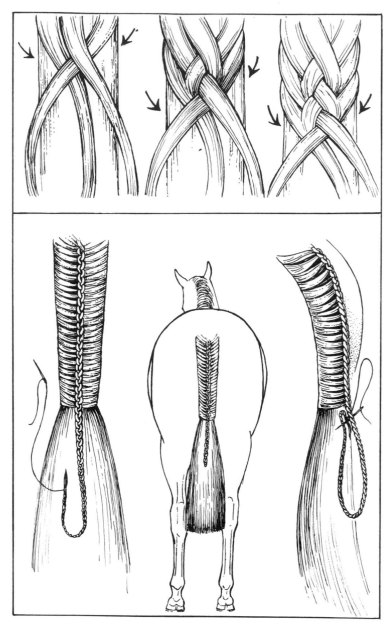

Plaiting the tail

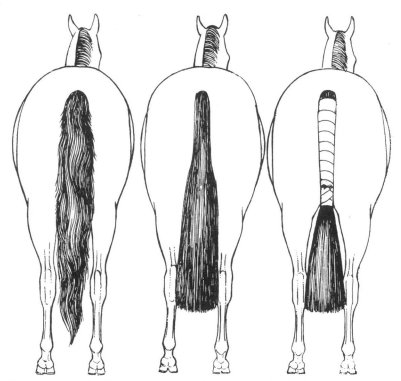

From the natural tail to the neatly bandaged squared-off tail

then to the left in a similar manner to hold the plait firmly. Pass the thread back down once more and knot, clipping off the thread neatly underneath. To undo, clip the side bindings and unroll being careful not to clip into the mane with the scissors. *Never* leave plaits in over night: get up at three in the morning to plait rather than doing so the night before, a practice by which many an owner has lost a section of mane.

TAILS If not pulled, tails are often plaited for special occasions. The ridge of the plait can either be inside or outside, the latter being harder to achieve but far smarter. To create a concealed ridge, plait overhand; for a raised ridge, plait underhand. In either case take a small section from the top of the tail on either side and a tiny bit from the centre to start the plait off. Now work down the tail taking in a fresh piece with each fold.

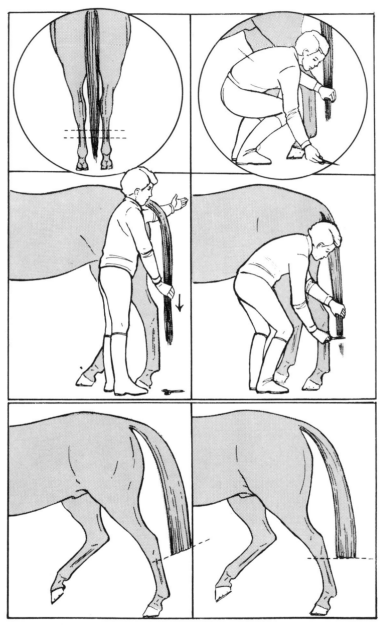

Squaring off the bottom of the tail

When low enough, stop gathering in extra hair and continue plaiting to the end adding a piece of thread a few inches from the bottom. Secure it as for the mane and then double up to hide the end under the last part of the plait across the tail, stitching the doubled-up plait down the centre to hold it. If the job has been well done, the result will be neat and attractive, but if badly done it is an eyesore.

Scissors and thinning combs have no place really in trimming a horse, except for squaring off the bottom of the tail or trimming the ears or heels. To square the bottom of the tail run your hand down from the dock to the end and, holding it firmly at the required length (level with the lowest part of the chestnut is about right), cut across. Release, brush out and repeat to get any stray hairs. Depending on how the horse carries its tail, angle the cut so that the tail is square to the ground when carried naturally.

Conclusion

There is an art to clipping, trimming and plaiting a horse properly but, as I have said earlier in this book, it is an art that an owner or groom can acquire. With practice and a working knowledge of the subject — a knowledge that I hope this book has gone some way to provide — and by application of care and patience, which are, of course, essential, a good result can be achieved. Some final reminders:

Remember to assemble your clipping equipment before starting and check the running of the clippers.

Ensure that your horse is dry and well groomed — a dirty, matted coat will not clip properly but will clog the clipper blades and make the horse sore and restless.

Clip steadily and do not force the clippers — if the coat is very thick, clip with coarse blades first, groom thoroughly and then reclip using normal blades. In this way the clippers will not be damaged by strain nor the horse made restless by pulling at the coat.

Check the clippers at frequent intervals against your own hand for heat and shocks. If they are too warm, turn them off and reoil. A horse, if never frightened, should soon take to clipping. Mine have always come rather to enjoy it, bar poor Gipsy — but that was the fault of the vandal with the gun!

Once your horse has been clipped, remember that *warmth* is *essential* for you have taken away its natural protection. When finished check for and treat any abrasions.